THE *Battle* OF *Bunker Hill*

An Interactive History Adventure

by Michael Burgan

Consultant:
Len Travers
Associate Professor of History
University of Massachusetts at Dartmouth

Mankato, Minnesota

You Choose Books are published by Capstone Press,
151 Good Counsel Drive, P.O. Box 669, Mankato, Minnesota 56002.
www.capstonepress.com

Library of Congress Cataloging-in-Publication Data
Burgan, Michael.
    The Battle of Bunker Hill: an interactive history adventure/
    by Michael Burgan.
    p. cm.—(You choose books)
    Includes bibliographical references and index.
    ISBN-13: 978-1-4296-0159-7 (hardcover)   ISBN-10: 1-4296-0159-0 (hardcover)
    ISBN-13: 978-1-4296-1178-7 (softcover)   ISBN-10: 1-4296-1178-2 (softcover)
1. Bunker Hill, Battle of, Boston, Mass., 1775—Juvenile literature. I. Title. II. Series.
E241.B9B97 2008
973.3'312—dc22   2007006942

Summary: Describes the events surrounding the Battle of Bunker Hill during the Revolutionary
    War. The reader's choices reveal the historical details from the perspective of a patriot soldier,
    a British soldier, and a Boston civilian.

Editorial Credits

Heather Adamson, editor; Juliette Peters, designer; Laura Manthe and Wanda Winch,
    photo researchers

Photo Credits

Anne S. K. Brown Military Collection, Brown University Library, 59; Art Resource, N.Y., 28; Art
Resource, N.Y./The New York Public Library, 19; The Bridgeman Art Library International/Private
Collection/A View of Part of the town of Boston in New England and British Ships of War Landing
Their Troops, 1768 (hand coloured print) Revere, Paul (1735–1818) (after), 101; The Bridgeman Art
Library/Courtesy of the Council, National Army Museum, London, UK, Bunker's Hill, 1775, c.1900
(w/c on paper), Simkin, Richard (1840–1926), 102, cover; Collection of the New-York Historical
Society, Uniforms of the American Revolution-52nd Regiment of Foot, by Charles M. Lefferts,
gouache, watercolor, accession number 1921.109., 66; Collection of the New-York Historical Society,
Uniforms of the American Revolution-American Farmers, by Charles M. Lefferts, gouache, watercolor,
accession number 1923.135., 82; Corbis/Bettmann, 6, 37, 96; Courtesy of Army Art Collection,
U.S. Army Center of Military History, 35; Getty Images Inc./Time & Life Pictures/Mansell, 48;
Library of Congress, 8, 54, 64; Maps.com, 10, 16; National Park Service, Harpers Ferry Center/artist
Don Troiani, 70; National Park Service, Harpers Ferry Center/artist Lloyd Kenneth Townsend,
44; New York Public Library, Emmet Collection, Miriam and Ira D. Wallach Div. of Art, Prints and
Photographs, Astor Lenox and Tilden Foundations, 33; New York Public Library, Picture Collection,
The Branch Libraries, Astor, Lenox and Tilden Foundations, 23; North Wind Picture Archives, 12, 40,
50, 61, 72, 80, 85, 87, 91; Pamela Patrick White/www.ppatrickwhite.com, 105

1 2 3 4 5 6 12 11 10 09 08 07

TABLE OF CONTENTS

About Your Adventure..5

Chapter 1:
  The Path to War...7
Chapter 2:
  Patriots: Pursuing Liberty.....................13
Chapter 3:
  British Soldiers:
  Keeping the Colonies......................45
Chapter 4:
  Life in Boston...73
Chapter 5:
  After the Battle......................................103

Time Line...106
Other Paths to Explore...108
Read More..109
Internet Sites...109
Glossary...110
Bibliography..111
Index..112

About Your Adventure

YOU are in Boston as the Revolutionary War begins. The British are attacking a patriot fort just outside the city. The city is divided between British Loyalists and American rebels. Which side are you on? And can you survive?

In this book, you'll explore how the choices people made meant the difference between life and death. The events you'll experience happened to real people.

Chapter One sets the scene. Then you choose which path to read. Follow the directions at the bottom of each page. The choices you make will change your outcome. After you finish one path, go back and read the others for new perspectives and more adventures.

YOU CHOOSE the path
you take through history.

American militia and British soldiers first battled near the towns of Lexington and Concord.

The Path to War

All of Boston buzzes with news from yesterday, April 19, 1775. British troops and American militia battled outside the city. You try to do what you normally do. But not much has been normal in Boston for a long time.

For almost seven years, British soldiers have been living in and around the city. The Americans call them "Redcoats" and "Lobsterbacks" because of the long red jackets they wear. The soldiers make sure the colonists follow the laws passed by the British parliament.

Turn the page.

The harbor made Boston a busy colonial port city.

It was different during the French and Indian War (1754–1763). Then King George's soldiers defended the colonies. Now, many colonists are tired of British control. For one thing, taxes keep going up and the colonists have no say. Some colonists want to break ties with the king. They call themselves patriots.

Other colonists like being British. These Loyalists think King George has a strong army and good trade ties. Loyalists wish the rebel patriots could work with the king.

In 1773, some patriots threw crates of tea into the harbor in protest of a tea tax. The British parliament responded with more laws. The relationship between the colonists and Britain has not improved.

On April 18, 1775, General Thomas Gage sent British troops to Concord. They tried to take patriot weapons and destroy battle supplies.

Patriots Paul Revere and William Dawes spread the word that British troops were coming. Patriots turned out to fight the British near Lexington and near Concord. No one knows who fired the first shot. But the battle raged all day.

Turn the page.

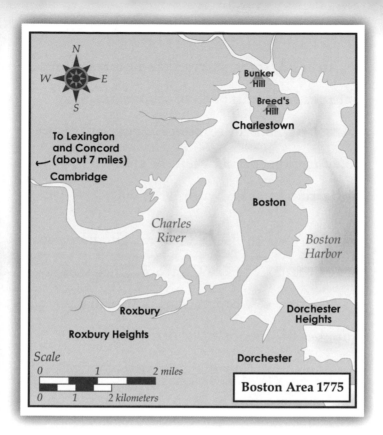

Boston Area 1775

Wounded British soldiers are still making their way to Boston. You hear the British soldiers talk. They are amazed the patriots fought so well. They are eager for revenge.

You also learn that thousands of patriot soldiers are coming. They're from across Massachusetts and parts of New England.

General Artemus Ward and his men are in Cambridge, just west of Charlestown. Patriot troops are also heading south to Roxbury. The patriots plan to start a siege of Boston. Goods and supplies will not be able to get into Boston. The British troops will be surrounded.

Of course, colonists living in Boston get most of their goods from British ships too. No one knows how life is going to change now that war has come to Boston. One thing is clear—another battle is coming soon. What will you do?

➠ *To fight in the Battle of Bunker Hill as a patriot soldier, turn to page* **13**.

➠ *To fight in the Battle of Bunker Hill as a British soldier, turn to page* **45**.

➠ *To see the Battle of Bunker Hill through a Boston civilian's eyes, turn to page* **73**.

Many patriot soldiers left their
farms to join the militia.

CHAPTER 2

Patriots:
Pursuing Liberty

You're not a professional soldier. Like most patriots, you're a simple farmer. But you want freedom from the British. After the Battles of Lexington and Concord, you decided to join the militia. You left Boston and went to train in Cambridge. For two months now, you have been training here.

It's evening now in Cambridge. Being away from your family and your farm is hard. You stay in a home that once belonged to a Loyalist. Many Loyalists fled Cambridge soon after the Lexington and Concord battles.

Turn the page.

You take some leftover bread from your pocket. Each day, patriot soldiers are given a pound of meat and a pound of bread. You sit down to eat a few slices and start writing a letter to your wife. You ask her to send a fresh shirt. All the marching drills and shooting practice dirties your clothes quickly. The day doesn't allow much time for washing. A clean, mended shirt would sure feel good.

You have heard that the British armies have women traveling with them. They mend and wash for the soldiers. That would be nice, but you wouldn't want your wife to be so close to danger.

On the morning street patrol, you overhear townspeople talking.

"Did you know General Gage is planning to move some Redcoats out of Boston?"

"Yes," the other replies, "I heard he plans to take them to Dorchester."

You know Dorchester is on high ground just south of Boston. The patriots would like control of that area. It would help in the siege of Boston. With a few cannons, patriots could trap British boats in the harbor. The British must not be allowed to take that hill.

Turn the page.

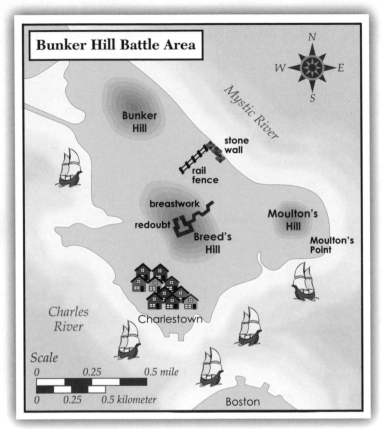

Bunker Hill Battle Area

N
W E
S

Mystic River

Bunker
Hill

stone
wall

rail
fence

breastwork

redoubt

Breed's
Hill

Moulton's
Hill

Moulton's
Point

Charlestown

*Charles
River*

Scale

0   0.25   0.5 mile

0   0.25   0.5 kilometer

Boston

By the time you return from patrol,
General Ward has orders for the patriots
to strike from the north first. Ward directs
Colonel William Prescott to lead about 1,000
men to Bunker Hill. The men will build a
small fort called a redoubt.

It's only a couple of miles march from Cambridge to the hill. But you will need to work fast. The British already have ships in the area. And it will not take long for the Redcoats in Boston to row across the half mile of water. Will you join Prescott in his mission?

➺ To go with the soldiers headed to Bunker Hill, turn to page **18**.

➺ To remain with the troops staying in Cambridge, turn to page **30**.

You carry your shovel and your musket. It's late on the night of June 16, 1775, and Colonel Prescott leads you and the others out of Cambridge. You meet up with 200 troops from Connecticut led by General Israel Putnam. Putnam, Prescott, and Richard Gridley, a military engineer, decide to send troops to Breed's Hill instead of Bunker Hill. It is closer to Boston.

Gridley outlines where the redoubt will go on the hill. You take your shovel and begin digging. The dirt forms the walls of the redoubt. Other men build a barrier called a breastwork. It extends beyond one of the walls. As you work, Colonel Prescott walks up and down the trenches. He tells you, "Faster—we must finish before sunrise. And be as quiet as possible! We don't want the British to know what we're doing."

Prescott and his men sneaked up Breed's Hill in the dark.

You haven't slept all night, and you haven't eaten since this afternoon. Your throat is dry, and you ache for water. But you ignore all that and obey Prescott's order. You dig as quietly as you can. You put your shovel into the earth over and over.

Turn the page.

Around 4:00 in the morning, a loud noise makes you look up. "Cannon fire!" a soldier cries, "From a ship in the harbor!"

The cannons fire again. Your friend Asa Pollard is working outside the redoubt wall. An iron cannon ball hits him. He's been killed. You and the other soldiers stand quiet. You're reminded that war has deadly consequences.

Colonel Prescott jumps up on the redoubt's dirt wall. "Come on, men," he yells. He ignores the cannon balls still flying through the air. "Keep working."

Some men have already left Breed's Hill. They have sneaked away when no one was looking. They fear a British attack on the redoubt. You're afraid too. But you know Colonel Prescott wants you to keep digging.

→ *If you follow Prescott's order and keep digging, turn to page 22.*

→ *If you ignore his order, turn to page 24.*

You keep digging as the sun rises in the sky. Throughout the morning, more patriot troops arrive. Some join the Connecticut troops, who have built a second breastwork of stone and wood. Troops from New Hampshire have also built a stone wall nearby. One of the new arrivals is Dr. Joseph Warren. He is a respected leader in Boston and a devoted patriot. You tell a friend, "If Dr. Warren is ready to risk his life here, then so am I."

All this time, British cannons fire. As the day goes on, you see small boats carrying Redcoats to the shore. Some climb out of the boats and begin marching toward Breed's Hill. Other troops head for the rail fence and the stone wall. The British will attack soon.

Dr. Joseph Warren (right) joined Prescott and the patriots at the redoubt.

➤ To defend the redoubt against the British troops, turn to page **32**.

➤ To face the British at the rail fence and stone wall, turn to page **39**.

You've changed your mind about fighting. Your family needs you back on the farm. You don't want to risk dying in battle.

When no one is looking, you drop your shovel and slowly move away from the redoubt. Looking around, you see other soldiers doing the same thing. You make your way back to Bunker Hill. A little later, you see men leaving Breed's Hill carrying shovels and picks.

"What's going on?" you ask.

"General Putnam wants us to build another breastwork here."

Some of the men begin to dig at Bunker Hill. Others, though, head past the hill and continue back toward Cambridge. You keep walking.

As you walk, you see more troops coming from Cambridge. They are heading toward the redoubt. They're ready to fight—and perhaps die—for the patriot cause. One calls out to you, "Where are you going? The British are going to land."

"I'm too tired," you reply. "I've been digging all night and I haven't had water for hours."

"That's no excuse," another soldier says. "Come with us."

➤ *If you continue to go Cambridge, turn to page 26.*

➤ *If you join the troops going to Breed's Hill, turn to page 29.*

The soldiers continue to stream past you, heading to Breed's Hill. The one who stopped you waits for an answer. "I can't go with you," you finally say. You look around. Other soldiers stream off the hill, looking for safety. Like you, they don't want to end up dead—like Asa Pollard. The British cannons still boom. Many men want to get as far from them as possible.

You continue walking to Cambridge. Some patriot soldiers come toward you, pulling four cannons. They are much smaller than the British guns pounding away at Breed's Hill. "We'll never stop the British with those puny cannons," you think to yourself.

Finally, with the hot June sun beating down, you reach town. You see more men preparing to march off to battle.

Others are trying to find wagons to bring supplies. Your stomach grumbles, reminding you that you haven't eaten yet today. You head for your camp, knowing your next meal is close by. But the men on Breed's Hill will have a long wait before they eat again.

You feel guilty that you left the battlefield. But you're eager to see your family again. You hope that the war will end soon, so you can go back to your regular life.

THE END

To follow another path, turn to page 11.
To read the conclusion, turn to page 103.

Patriot soldiers waited for the British to march up the hill.

You turn around and join the men marching toward Breed's Hill. You believe in the patriot cause of freedom. You are tired and thirsty, but want to do your part. You are glad to see that a lot of work has gone on since the early morning.

A stone wall and a rail fence form a breastwork that runs from the Mystic River toward the redoubt. Men from New Hampshire and Connecticut stand ready at these posts. Regiments from Massachusetts head to the redoubt and the breastwork right near it.

Turn to page 32.

You watch the men go off to Bunker Hill. Then you go to bed. On the morning of June 17, the distant sound of booming cannons wakes you up early. British ships in the harbor are firing on Charlestown. You check your musket and wait with the other soldiers. You know General Ward is at his headquarters, waiting for news from Colonel Prescott.

The soldiers wonder what will happen.

"The Redcoats will attack Cambridge," one says. "Ward has got to keep us here."

"But those men on Bunker Hill can't go it alone," you reply. "He has to send more troops."

Soon General Ward decides to send some New Hampshire men to help Prescott. Prescott and his men have actually built the redoubt on Breed's Hill instead of Bunker Hill. The New Hampshire troops have built a stone wall near the Mystic River, north of the redoubt. Connecticut and Massachusetts regiments head to the redoubt. In either place, the fighting could be fierce.

➼ *To join the Massachusetts regiments at the redoubt on Breed's Hill, turn to page 32.*

➼ *To join the New Hampshire regiments at the stone wall, turn to page 39.*

The redoubt is small, but the walls are thick. This fort will provide good defense against the British soldiers who have started their march from the beach.

It's now about 3:30 in the afternoon, and the June sun is beating down on you. The temperature has soared to 95 degrees. Your broad-brimmed hat helps keep the sun's heat off your face. You see a wave of British soldiers head toward a rail fence where the Connecticut troops are hiding in the grass. The Redcoats also don't seem to see the New Hampshire regiment. They are behind a stone wall they built this morning from tide rocks. The patriots open fire quickly, killing several dozen British troops.

Patriots worked through the night to build a strong redoubt.

At the same time, a group of Redcoats has made it up through the tall grass and over the rocky ground. They are nearing your position in the redoubt. You quickly pack your musket with gunpowder and a lead ball.

Turn the page.

"Fire!" Colonel Prescott shouts.

You pull the trigger, and your musket jerks upward in your hands. Other guns around you go off at the same time. Clouds of smoke form from the exploding gunpowder. Many of the British have been hit. You reload your musket and fire again. Dozens of dead British soldiers now lie around the redoubt.

You join the other men in a cheer, as the British stopped their advance. But a larger force soon heads toward the redoubt. You go to reload again, but a sharp, hot pain fills your arm.

"I've been hit," you cry.

A soldier at your side helps wrap a cloth around your wound. As you sit down, you see that the British have retreated again. But no one thinks they have given up.

Soldiers used their guns as clubs and swords when they got close to the enemy.

Around you, the patriots reload their muskets. Someone tells you to leave the redoubt and retreat back to Bunker Hill. You want to stay and fight, but the pain is getting worse.

➻ If you stay to continue fighting, turn to page **36**.

➻ If you decide to retreat, turn to page **43**.

Staying to fight is the honorable thing to do, you decide. Your arm hurts too much for you to hold your gun, but you help bring gunpowder to some men who have run out. The supplies are now almost gone. You search the ground for nails or other bits of metal that the others can fire from their guns.

Only about an hour has passed since the fighting started. But to you it feels like days. Around 4:30 in the afternoon, you see the British advance a third time. They march in a single rank. The patriots fire the nails. Others throw rocks. But nothing stops the British this time. They charge over the redoubt walls. They stab the men around you with their bayonets. Men you have trained with for weeks are now dead at your feet.

Dr. Joseph Warren was shot while defending the redoubt.

Some of the patriots begin to run toward Bunker Hill. Others keep fighting even as the British pour over the wall. Colonel Prescott uses his sword to push away enemy bayonets. You quickly try to crawl away. You turn and see Dr. Warren leaving the redoubt. A British soldier shoots the brave leader. He falls to the ground.

Turn the page.

In the same moment, a British soldier lunges at you with his bayonet. You've been stabbed in the heart. As you take your last breath, you know have given your life for the great cause of American freedom.

THE END

To follow another path, turn to page 11.
To read the conclusion, turn to page 103.

The morning low tide exposed a lot of stone and rock. Patriots quickly piled it together to form another defense. The stone wall extends to a nearby rail fence overgrown with grass. The stone wall and fence should keep the British from just going around the redoubt.

You take your place behind the stone wall. Soon, Colonel John Stark gives orders to prepare for a British attack. You pack gunpowder and a lead ball into your musket. Colonel Stark jumps over the wall. He walks about 40 yards out and drives a stake in the ground. When he returns he says, "Not a man is to fire until the first Redcoat crosses the stake." Stark wants to make sure you will not waste ammunition. You must hit your targets.

Turn the page.

Hundreds of British troops have now landed on the beach. They leave their boats and approach the wall. Fifteen Redcoats march side by side, 20 rows deep. As they pass the stake in the ground, Stark motions for you to fire. You pull the trigger and feel the kick from your musket. All around you, other guns go off at the same time.

The patriots shot down the British soldiers one row at a time.

You look through the cloud of smoke from the guns. British soldiers lie dead or dying. Still, others keep marching toward the wall.

Another group of patriot soldiers fires their guns, and then a third. With each round of firing, more Redcoats fall to the ground. The troops behind them can't move past the bodies, and they begin to retreat.

The patriots at the redoubt are also driving off the British. You hear their cheer of success and you feel good too. Colonel Stark walks along the wall. He says, "The fighting's not done yet, lads. The Redcoats will be back."

Soon you see Stark is right. The British attack the rail fence near the stone wall. You fire at them, as do the defenders at the fence. Once again, the British quickly retreat.

Turn the page.

Sweat rolls down your face. You have been in the sun for hours. Around 4:30 in the afternoon, another group of Redcoats starts coming toward the stone wall. A much larger force is also attacking the redoubt.

As you reload your musket, a shot hits you in the arm. As you slump down, you see the British storm the redoubt. The patriots there begin to retreat to Bunker Hill. Colonel Stark orders all of you to retreat as well.

Holding your wounded arm, you retreat to Bunker Hill. Patriots there have dug trenches as another line of defense. You watch the patriot defenses crumble at the Breed's Hill redoubt. The British soon attack Bunker Hill. "Stand and give them one more shot," General Putnam cries.

It is no use. The British soon overrun Bunker Hill too. The patriots retreat further. But the British troops do not follow. They have taken the redoubt. And they have lost too many men to keep fighting.

That night, a doctor treats your wound. You can only think that the patriots have lost badly at the Battle of Bunker Hill. But you and the patriots will not quit the fight for freedom.

THE END

To follow another path, turn to page 11.
To read the conclusion, turn to page 103.

European battle style had
soldiers march in rows.

CHAPTER 3

British Soldiers: Keeping the Colonies

At sunrise on the morning of June 17, you wake to the sound of cannon fire. Even from your quarters in Boston, the noise is enough to get your attention.

"It's our ships," someone says. "They're firing on the colonist rebels." Overnight, the rebels began building a small fort called a redoubt. The fort is on a hill near Charlestown.

45

For weeks you've waited for another chance to fight the rebel Americans. You still see the image of your friends dying on the way back from Concord. Since then, several thousand British soldiers have arrived from England.

Turn the page.

"Prepare for battle!" The order comes down from your regiment leader. You put on your red coat and tall, pointed black hat. You tie up your long hair with a ribbon. Next you strap on belts that hold your bayonet and the cartridges for your gun. Then you sling over your back the pack that holds extra clothes, food, water, and other supplies.

It takes nearly three hours to organize all the soldiers for fighting. You're ready to get to the battle.

General William Howe will lead the first attack on Charlestown. General Henry Clinton will remain behind and command reinforcements.

➤ To follow the soldiers who go with Howe, go on to page **47**.

➤ To follow the reinforcements under Clinton, turn to page **60**.

It's about noon as your regiment boards a rowboat. You count another 27 boats in the water from Boston to Charlestown, less than a half mile away. The boats head for a spot called Moulton's Point. British ships keep firing cannons to keep the beach clear of rebels.

By 3:00 in the afternoon, all the men have crossed the water. General Howe divides his forces. He takes your regiment and several others to attack a stone wall and rail fence north of the redoubt. General Robert Pigot heads left toward the fort itself. As Pigot's men march away, shots ring out from some buildings in Charlestown. Rebel shooters are hiding there. Howe orders the town destroyed and set on fire. As you march into battle, you see smoke begin to rise from the town.

Turn the page.

The British set fire to Charlestown so patriot snipers could not attack them.

Drums play as you march side-by-side with the other soldiers. Ahead and behind you are more rows of British troops. You move slowly. The ground is covered with rocks and holes that you can't easily see in the tall grass. The pack on your back weighs at least 60 pounds. It feels extra heavy because of the hot June sun. Still, the guns from the British ships keep booming. You keep marching toward the wall.

Suddenly, as you near the wall, the rebels begin to fire. You see men ahead of you fall to the ground. Some are dead. Some are wounded. A sergeant near you shouts, "Come on, soldiers, keep marching!"

You watch as men around you are shot and killed. You could be killed too if you keep moving. But if you don't follow orders, you could be whipped as punishment. What do you do?

49

➤ *If you turn back, turn to page* **50**.

➤ *If you keep marching, turn to page* **54**.

Long grass, bumpy ground, and dead bodies made it hard for the Redcoats to keep marching.

The sight of all the dead soldiers is too much to bear. You break out of the line and run across the field. Your foot catches in a hole. You fall and hit your head on a stone. You feel blood on your head, but you get up and run.

On the shore, you see other infantrymen who have fled the battle. Some have wounds. Most are scared.

They never thought the rebels could shoot so well. Some of the men crowd into the boats hoping to hide. Officers come by, yelling "Get out, you cowards! This battle isn't over yet."

One officer pushes you with his sword. "You too, soldier. You're going again. General Howe wants to make another go at the fence."

You point at the wound on your head. "I've been shot," you lie. "I need to go back to Boston."

The officer looks at you closely. "There are men still out there with worse injuries. Are you that much of a coward?"

➤ *If you still don't want to fight, turn to page* **52**.

➤ *If you decide to fight, turn to page* **53**.

"I . . . I'm not a coward," you say. "But this wound . . ."

"All right, all right," the officer says with disgust. "Get on the boat."

Within a few minutes, the boat is filled with wounded men. Some moan in pain. Others are barely alive. As you sail toward Boston, you hear the sound of guns and see the sky fill with smoke. Perhaps you were a coward. But at least you are alive.

THE END

To follow another path, turn to page 11.
To read the conclusion, turn to page 103.

You start to feel bad about running away from the battle. Men you know have died bravely, while you're afraid to do your duty. You decide that you must act with honor. If you don't keep your service to the king, you are no better than the rebel colonists.

"Maybe the wound is not so bad after all," you say.

"I thought so," the officer said. "Go on, get out there."

You head back to the beach where most of the men are waiting for orders. You prepare for another attack on the fence.

Turn to page **58**.

British soldiers assembled on the beach between their attacks on Breed's Hill.

The rebel guns continue to fire as you move forward. At times, you step across dead British soldiers who were your friends. You hear an order to stop and fire. Your shot has no effect, as the rebel soldiers are safely behind the wall and fence.

As you reach for another cartridge for your gun, an officer calls out, "Pull back! Back to the beach!"

You turn to run and cross back over the rocky ground. A voice screams, "Help! Help me!"

You look down and see a soldier from your regiment. He is lying on the ground. Blood flows from his chest.

"Help me," he begs. "I'll never make it back to the boats alone."

The rebel guns are still firing. If you stop to help, you could be killed. But you know you would want someone to help you if you were wounded.

➤ *To help the soldier, turn to page 56.*
➤ *To keep retreating, turn to page 58.*

The wounded soldier stares up at you.
He is pleading.

"All right, hold on," you say.

You kneel by the soldier to help him up.
His clothes are soaked with blood. You struggle
to your feet, holding him with your right arm.
Slowly you begin to half-drag and half-carry
him across the field. After only a few steps,
you feel a hot, piercing pain in your left leg.

"I'm shot!" you cry.

You struggle to keep your balance. The pain
makes your head pound. The wounded soldier
is getting weaker. He starts to drag his feet.

"Come on," you say. "We can make it."

After a few minutes, you see the boats on the shore. The soldier is still breathing, but just barely. Blood is still flowing from your wound, but you think you can reach the boat. Now you hope you live until you reach the hospital back in Boston.

THE END

To follow another path, turn to page 11.
To read the conclusion, turn to page 103.

On the beach, you see General Howe. He is stunned at the losses and the rebel defense. Within 15 minutes, Howe has prepared those left for another attack on the fence. Your regiment begins marching again.

Once again, you march in line. Fifes and drums play as you walk over and around the men who have already died. The order comes, "Prepare for a bayonet charge."

As you wait for the order to charge, a rebel officer yells, "Fire!" Gunshots break out. Soldiers once again fall around you. You move to the side, but the rebels continue to fire. General Howe stands in the middle of the smoke and bloodshed.

"Once more, men," he cries, "once more. "Show them what British soldiers can do."

General Howe was surprised at how well the patriots defended Breed's Hill.

The enemy fire is too heavy for you to reach the fence and use your bayonet. You decide to stop and shoot instead. You take aim at one of the defenders behind a rail. The shot hits its target. Before you can reload, a musket ball strikes you. You are killed instantly.

THE END

To follow another path, turn to page 11.
To read the conclusion, turn to page 103.

You wait in Boston for your orders to sail. Boats full of wounded soldiers keep returning across the harbor. These men were hit during in first attack on the redoubt. You help carry the men. You hear hundreds of guns fire during a second attack. Then there is silence, except for the booming of cannons and the cries of more men in pain.

Around 4:00 in the afternoon, General Clinton orders your regiment to sail to Moulton's Point. General Clinton climbs into the lead boat. As the boats approach the shore, musket balls are fired at you. Several men in General Clinton's boat are shot. General Clinton ignores the gunfire. He jumps onto the shore. He sends some of the men to support General Howe at Breed's Hill. General Clinton takes command of everyone else on the beach.

The fighting on Breed's Hill was more fierce than most soldiers were expecting.

⇢ To fight under Clinton's command, turn to page **62**.

⇢ To go help fight under Howe's command, turn to page **64**.

General Clinton begins organizing the men on the beach. He also calls out to the men wounded in the earlier battles.

"I know you've advanced two times already. And we've suffered great losses. But we must take that redoubt! If you can walk and hold a gun, follow me."

You help one or two of the wounded struggle to their feet. General Clinton forms all the soldiers into lines on the beach. You will help General Robert Pigot, who has been attacking the redoubt.

Pigot's men have already suffered heavy casualties during the two attacks. At 4:30 in the afternoon, the third attack on the redoubt begins. Your rank marches past dead British soldiers. You know your own life could end at any moment. But you will fight to the end. The order comes to prepare for a bayonet charge. Other soldiers fall in front of you, hit by rebel gunfire. But you keep running and reach the wall of the redoubt.

Turn to page 66.

Despite the heavy losses, British soldiers continued to attack.

For the first two attacks, the men carried their heavy packs. This time, you are told to leave your packs behind. Without the extra weight, you'll be able to move more easily. Some of the men take off their red coats as well. It helps to ease the blistering heat.

You look out over the field you must cross to reach the redoubt. Dead British soldiers lie in heaps. The drums begin to play. You march out toward the rebels. Rebel shots take down some of the men in front. Others step up to take their place.

The British artillery keeps firing at the small fort. Smoke from exploding gunpowder floats over the field. "Push on, push on!" some soldiers holler around you. You attach your bayonet blade to the end of your gun.

Turn the page.

British soldiers attached long blades called bayonets to their guns.

You climb over the wall of the redoubt with your bayonet in front of you. The rebels are running out of ammunition. An American swings at your head with his musket. You use your bayonet to fight off the patriot.

British soldiers are storming into the redoubt from three sides. Many of the rebels flee. Others lay dead on the ground. You turn to attack a rebel before he can escape. At that moment, you feel a powerful thud. The clubbing blow drops you to your knees in pain. You struggle to your feet. Touching the side of your head, you feel blood. Angry, you want to keep fighting. But you know you could be killed if you can't defend yourself.

67

➻ If you keep fighting, turn to page **68**.

➻ If you seek help for your wound, turn to page **70**.

You don't have to worry about another rebel hitting you. As you look around, you see only British troops left in the redoubt. The rebels are running back to Bunker Hill. You join troops chasing the enemy.

A few rebel shots fire as you near Bunker Hill. You charge with your bayonet. The rebels retreat off of the hill. Soon, the British soldiers have control of Bunker Hill as well.

You help some men bring cannons to the top of the hill. The guns fire at the retreating rebels. British ships also aim at the rebels as they flee. The battle is over, but your day is not. You have orders to begin building a new fort on Bunker Hill. The war against the rebels is just beginning.

THE END

To follow another path, turn to page 11.
To read the conclusion, turn to page 103.

Wounded British soldiers were brought to Boston all through the night.

You climb out of the redoubt and walk back toward the beach. Another soldier helps you bandage your head. You see that you're lucky. Many of the men have worse wounds than you. You board a boat to cross the harbor. The bottom is covered in blood from the other wounded men it has already carried today.

You reach the docks in Boston. Wagons are waiting. Civilians have come out to help bring the wounded to hospitals. Even wheelbarrows are used to carry the injured men.

You're able to walk to the hospital. Along the way, you see your sergeant. His arm is in a sling.

"Are you all right, soldier?" he asks.

"Yes, Sergeant. And you?"

He holds up the injured arm. "Not too bad. Just missing a bit of flesh."

"How did we do, sir?" you ask.

"We won the battle today, but this war is far from over."

You keep walking, wondering if you will be lucky enough to survive another battle like this one.

THE END

To follow another path, turn to page 11.
To read the conclusion, turn to page 103.

British soldiers occupied Boston and tried to enforce laws passed by the British parliament.

CHAPTER 4

Life in Boston

You see many changes in Boston in the weeks after the battle of April 19, 1775. Some of your friends have left the city. They fear the patriots will attack the Redcoats in Boston. At the same time, several thousand Loyalists stream into the capital. Patriots forced them from their homes because they support the British. The Loyalists believe they'll be safe in Boston. The British guns can protect them.

You're still not sure what you and your family should do. Your best friend decides to help the patriots.

Turn the page.

"Come with me," your friend says. "Bring your family and all that you can carry in your wagon. Get out of Boston."

"I don't know," you say. "You really think the patriots are fighting for a good cause?"

"Of course," he says. "They're fighting to protect our liberty. We can't elect our own leaders, like we always did before. And don't forget the laws they passed after the tea went in the harbor—the Intolerable Acts."

"That's true," you reply. "I've been worrying about being told to house British soldiers."

"Only the patriots," says your friend, "will make sure we have our rights again. The king and his men—they don't care about us over here in America."

"The British government is the best in the world," you say. "We still have plenty of freedom."

You friend shakes his head. "If the patriots lose, the British will keep taking away more rights. I'm going to Cambridge to fight for our liberty."

➤ To support the patriots, turn to page **76**.

➤ To be a Loyalist in support of the British, turn to page **88**.

You decide that your friend is right. But you're not ready to leave Boston. You fear Loyalists or thieves will take what you leave behind. You send your family to Cambridge. They'll be safer there. Any fighting will likely be closer to the harbor. And with the patriot siege, goods are only going to get harder to find.

In June, you go out to a local tavern with some friends. "I heard some Redcoats talking," says one friend. "They think they'll be sent to Dorchester soon."

"The patriots need to control Dorchester," you say. "With a few large cannons, they could trap British boats in the harbor." If the British take Dorchester, the patriot siege of Boston would be unsuccessful.

You know that the patriots need this information. But you have no safe way to get out of Boston. General Gage will not approve travel passes for patriots to leave the city. If you try to sneak out, you could be arrested.

➻ To leave Boston and give the patriots the information, turn to page **78**.

➻ To stay in Boston, turn to page **86**.

You decide the information is worth the risk. You dress as a fisherman and borrow a friend's rowboat. At nightfall, you cross the water. Luckily, no soldiers are along the shore. You head for Charlestown, since the town is almost empty. Most people have left in case more fighting breaks out. You walk the 3 miles from Charlestown to Cambridge. When you reach town, you see a patriot officer and give him your information.

The next day, you travel through Roxbury and across the Boston Neck. As you enter the city, some Loyalists recognize you. They know you are a patriot and should not have been allowed out of Boston. One of the men starts talking to a soldier on Cornhill Street. You turn around and begin to walk quickly in the other direction.

"Halt!" the soldier commands. You stop. With his large black hat, the soldier seems to tower over you.

"Were you just outside Boston?" the soldier asks. "Tell me what you were doing."

You look up at the officer and lie. "My family is in Cambridge. My son is sick. I need to see him."

"All right," the officer says. "You may go."

As you walk away, you see the Loyalists glaring at you. You know they will be watching you closely. You decide you must leave Boston. That night, you leave for Cambridge again. But this time, you won't come back to Boston.

Turn the page.

Colonial women feared losing their husbands in battle.

You find your family. They are staying with a group of friends from Boston. "You should join our regiment and fight with us," one man says.

"Who would take care of my wife and children?" you say. "I'd have to leave my family."

"Yes, we all have families. Fighting this war is the only way to protect our freedom," another adds.

You look over at your wife. She is almost crying. She fears being alone if you're killed in battle. Yet you know how important it is to defeat the British.

➤ If you decide to fight, turn to page 82.

➤ If you decide not to fight, turn to page 84.

Unlike the British soldiers, patriots did not wear the same uniforms until later in the war.

You hug your wife before heading off. You tell her, "I must do my part, dear. I must fight."

You are welcomed into the regiment, but they don't have a musket for you. The patriots are low on many supplies, including guns. The troops stay together in crowded houses. Some sleep outside in tents made from old sails.

Later, 800 Massachusetts troops head to Cambridge. They gather there and then head toward Charlestown. "Where are they going?" you ask an officer.

"Bunker Hill," he replies. "We're going to make the first move—before the British attack Dorchester."

The sound of British cannons wakes you early on June 17, 1775. As the day goes on, more men are sent to Breed's Hill and Bunker Hill. Your regiment will stay in Cambridge.

At the day's end, dirty, bloody men march back to Cambridge. They tell you they didn't have enough ammunition. Many men died, but you know the war has just begun.

THE END

To follow another path, turn to page 11.
To read the conclusion, turn to page 103.

You look at your wife again. You tell your friends you don't want to fight. Your friends look angry. They leave without saying anything.

Soon a larger group comes to the door. "You say you won't fight," one man says. "How do we know you're really a patriot?"

"You could be a Loyalist spy," another says. "If you were one of us, you would have left Boston long before now."

"I'm a patriot," you say. "But my family—"

"We all have families. But we're doing what's right. Maybe you and your family should leave."

The crowd is getting angrier. You fear for your safety. You tell your wife and children to gather whatever they can carry. You leave quickly.

"Go on, coward," someone calls. "Go back to the Loyalists."

Some Loyalists were run out of town by the patriots.

You think Boston is too dangerous now. You decide to stay with relatives in Springfield. The trip will take about 10 days over rough roads, but at least you'll be safe there.

85

THE END

To follow another path, turn to page 11.
To read the conclusion, turn to page 103.

You decide not to risk leaving Boston. You hope someone else will tell General Ward about the British plans.

On the morning of June 17, you wake early in the morning to the sound of cannons firing. You learn the patriots have built a small fort called a redoubt on Breed's Hill. They worked through the night. British ships have just spotted it now in the daylight.

By noon, you watch the Redcoats gather at the Long Wharf docks. The soldiers climb into boats and begin to cross to Charlestown. Well-dressed Loyalists and other citizens stream by you. They head for the highest hills in the city.

"Where are you going?" you call to a woman.

People in Boston climbed on rooftops to get a good view.

"To watch the battle. You can see the troops from the hills." Breed's Hill is just a half mile away, and the day is clear. It will be easy to watch the battle.

Turn to page 97.

Even though you don't like some of the things the king and his government have done in the colonies, you remain loyal to him. You decide to stay in Boston and support the British.

During the next few weeks, food and other supplies run low in Boston. The patriots guard all the roads into the city. They allow very little food to come in. Some Loyalists are able to sneak in food from relatives outside the city. You don't have any relatives who can help. You must pay the high prices charged in the shops.

You can't afford much cheese or bread. For most meals, you eat salted meat and peas.

On June 12, General Gage declares patriots "rebels and traitors." Still, he is willing to pardon any of them who turn in their guns.

A few days later, a British officer comes to you.

"You call yourself a loyal citizen of Great Britain?" he asks.

"Yes sir," you reply. "The patriots are breaking the law."

"Then maybe you can help us. We're asking several Loyalists to go to Cambridge. We want to find out what the patriots are doing."

"You mean you want me to spy?"

"Exactly," the officer says.

You want to help the British defeat the patriots. And if you say no to the officer, he might think you're not truly loyal to the king. But spying is dangerous. If you are caught, the patriots will arrest you—or worse.

→ *To agree to help spy, turn to page* **90**.

→ *If you don't want to spy, turn to page* **99**.

The officer gives you a pass so you can leave Boston. On the morning of June 16, you walk down Cornhill Street and across Boston Neck. From there, you walk to Cambridge. When you arrive there, you see patriot troops gathering in the center of the city. They wear the same broad hats and simple clothes they wore on their farms. The Redcoats, you think, certainly look more like real soldiers.

You spot a Loyalist you knew in Boston. He fled the city right after the Battle of Lexington and Concord.

"What's going on?" you ask him.

"I'm not sure," he replies. "But it looks like they're getting ready to march somewhere. Perhaps to Charlestown."

"I have to get back to Boston and tell the British," you say.

Patriot troops gathered in Cambridge before heading to Breed's Hill and Bunker Hill.

"It will be faster by boat," the Loyalist says. "I know someone who might be able to help."

The two of you head for the water. On the way, a patriot patrol stops you.

"Where are you two going?" one of the men asks.

Turn the page.

"And who are you?" another demands, sticking his musket into your chest.

"I'm visiting family here in Cambridge," you lie. "I've been staying in Boston to protect our home from the Loyalists."

"Are you sure you're not a Loyalist yourself?" the first man asks. "Maybe even a spy?"

You feel your hands begin to sweat. You could try to lie again, but they might not believe you. Or you could try to run.

→ To run, go on to page **93**.

→ To try lying again, turn to page **95**.

You decide to run. You bolt off the road and head into some nearby woods.

"Halt!" the soldiers cry. One of them fires his gun over your head. You keep running, but you don't see a rock in your path. You trip over it and tumble to the ground. Before you can get up again, one of the soldiers is standing above you. His gun is pointed at your chest.

"Not a Loyalist, eh?" he sneers. "You liar. Come on."

The other soldier is guarding your friend. A crowd begins to form as they march you through town.

"What have we here?" someone asks the soldiers. "No-good Loyalists?"

"This one's a spy," the soldier says.

Turn the page.

"Tar and feather them!" another person calls out. You cringe. Just a year before, you watched a mob tear off the clothes of a man cover his body with hot tar and feathers.

"We're bringing them to jail," one of the soldiers says. The guards throw you and your friend into a tiny cell.

The next morning, you hear the distant sound of battle. The patriot troops you had seen yesterday did go to Charlestown, and the British attacked them there.

THE END

To follow another path, turn to page 11.
To read the conclusion, turn to page 103.

You tell the soldier again that you were just here to see your family.

The soldier pokes his gun in your chest and looks you in the eye.

"Alright," he says, "but we'll be watching you. You'd better not be heading back to Boston today."

You and your friend are quite relieved to have been let go. You decide not to risk heading to Boston tonight. You know you will probably not get your information to the British in time. Still, you think you will be safer in Boston with the other Loyalists.

As the sun comes up, you start your walk to Boston. A boat would be faster, but going by land through Roxbury is less risky. It takes you a few hours to walk to Boston.

Turn the page.

As you get nearer to the city, you can hear cannons firing in the harbor. You know the battle has begun. As you enter town, people are still talking about the fort that the patriots built on Breed's Hill. You see lots of townspeople walking toward Beacon Hill. It is a clear day. From the hill, you will be able to watch the battle on Breed's Hill.

Breed's Hill was a half mile from Boston. Citizens climbed on roofs to watch the battle.

You join the crowd of people heading up Beacon Hill. People are climbing onto rooftops. They even sit on the pointed steeples of churches.

The British troops make their way toward a rail fence and stone wall near the redoubt. They move slowly, because the ground in front of them is rocky and covered with tall grass. They carry large packs on their backs.

You know the patriots are waiting behind the fence and wall. The soldiers look like tiny toys, but you know what you're watching is real. The British advance, and the Americans fire. Rows of Redcoats fall to the ground, dead or wounded.

Smoke starts to rise from Charlestown. The town is on fire, most likely set by the British.

Turn the page.

As the fighting goes on, your stomach turns a bit. You never wanted things to come to bloodshed.

Your legs ache. The clock tower at the Old South Meeting House reads just past 4:30. You've been standing on the hill for two hours.

British reinforcements arrive from Charlestown. They are going to make another charge. They storm the redoubt. Soon, you see patriots fleeing the fort on Breed's Hill. A wave of Redcoats chases them off Bunker Hill as well.

By 5:00 in the afternoon, the British have won control of the hills. The battle is over, but the war has just begun.

THE END

To follow another path, turn to page 11.
To read the conclusion, turn to page 103.

"I want to help," you tell the officer, "but I don't want to be a spy. Perhaps I can join the Loyal American Associators."

"We need spies, not guards," he mutters.

You head off to find General Timothy Ruggles, the leader of the Loyal American Associators. He founded the group so Boston Loyalists could help the British defend the city. You can't find Ruggles, but you find one of the officers.

"Here's a musket," he says. "We'll be training tomorrow."

"I thought everyone in the city had turned in their weapons," you say.

"Not us. We can help defend the city if the rebels attack."

Turn the page.

On June 17, General Ruggles meets with the other British generals. They plan their response to a rebel fort built in the night. The British decide to attack the redoubt. You wonder if you will fight too. But when the battle begins that afternoon, you and the other Loyalist militia remain in Boston.

As the day goes on, you see smoke rising from the battlefield and the city of Charlestown. You're told to go to the docks at Long Wharf. Boats are carrying the wounded British soldiers back to Boston. You rush to get your wagon. Soon, the streets around the docks are filled with other wagons, carts, and wheelbarrows. You help carry the wounded. The moans of the injured fill your ears. Your hands are covered with blood.

"Work quickly," one officer says. "We have more boats coming in."

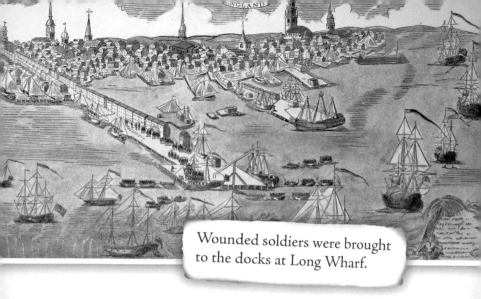

Wounded soldiers were brought to the docks at Long Wharf.

You help pull a wagon of wounded to the hospital. Then you return to the docks for another load. You do this over and over. The boats keep coming all night. Many of the soldiers die. You help bury them in the graveyards around Boston. You hope that the war ends quickly. You don't want anyone digging a grave for you anytime soon.

THE END

To follow another path, turn to page 11.
To read the conclusion, turn to page 103.

The battle on Breed's Hill
lasted about two hours.

CHAPTER 5

After the Battle

When the fighting was over on June 17, 1775, the British had won the battle. After the first two British attacks on the redoubt at Breed's Hill, the patriots ran out of ammunition. With their third attack, the Redcoats forced the patriots to flee and retreat to Cambridge.

But the British paid a high price for their victory. They had 226 men killed and 800 other wounded out of 2,200 men. The patriots had just 140 killed and 271 wounded of 1,500 men.

Even with those losses, General Clinton was eager to fight again. He wanted to attack Dorchester within a week, but General Gage refused.

Instead, Gage asked for more troops to defend Boston. After the loss, British generals decided to change their strategy. No more attacks on rebels behind well-built redoubts.

For the Americans, the death of Dr. Warren was a great loss. Patriots respected his courage and loyalty. There were rumors of his last words. People said Warren told the patriots to "fight on, my brave fellows."

Other stories spread about an order General Putnam gave his troops. He said, "Don't fire until you see the whites of their eyes." Today, many historians think those words are just a legend.

While the Battle of Bunker Hill was going on, patriot leaders formed the Second Continental Congress. They chose George Washington to command the patriot forces.

Patriot militias joined the Continental Army after the Battle of Bunker Hill.

The next March, Washington placed cannons on Dorchester Heights. Washington knew an attack could destroy Boston. So, he decided to let the British leave the city. By March 17, 1776, the siege of Boston was over.

The Revolutionary War, however, had just begun. In July, the Second Continental Congress approved the Declaration of Independence. The colonists were now fighting for the right to form their own country. The battle for independence lasted for almost seven more years. In 1783, the Americans finally won their independence from the British.

Time Line

October 1768—British troops arrive in Boston to keep order in the city.

December 1773—To protest a tax on tea, patriots throw crates of tea into Boston Harbor; this event is soon called the Boston Tea Party.

April 18, 1775—General Gage sends British troops to Concord, Massachusetts, to seize weapons the patriots have stored there.

April 19, 1775—Patriots and British soldiers fight in Lexington and Concord, marking the start of the Revolutionary War.

April 20, 1775—Thousands of patriot militia from across New England come to the Boston area to prepare for more battles with British soldiers.

May 1775—Patriot leaders from the 13 colonies meet together in Philadelphia at the Second Continental Congress.

June 15, 1775—The patriots learn about British plans to attack Dorchester, south of Boston. Patriots decide they'd rather make the first move and plan an attack from the north.

June 16, 1775—In the cover of night, Colonel William Prescott leads 1,000 men to Charlestown. They are to build a redoubt on Bunker Hill.

June 17, 1775 12:00 a.m.—Patriots decide to build the fort on nearby Breed's Hill instead. They begin digging and building as quietly as possible.

4:00 a.m.—The British awake to see the American activity on Breed's Hill. They begin firing ship cannons and assembling troops.

3:30 p.m.—British soldiers form their lines and begin first attack on the redoubt.

4:00 p.m.—British make a second attempt to take the redoubt.

4:30 p.m.—The British soldiers make a third attack. It is successful. They have won the Battle of Bunker Hill but suffer heavy losses.

March 1776—Patriots bring cannons to Dorchester. British troops withdraw to Nova Scotia. The siege of Boston ends.

September 1783—The Treaty of Paris is signed, officially ending the American Revolution.

OTHER PATHS TO EXPLORE

In this book, you've seen how the events surrounding the Battle of Bunker Hill look different from three points of view.

Perspectives on history are as varied as the people who lived it. You can explore other paths on your own to learn more about what happened. Seeing history from many points of view is an important part of understanding it.

Here are some ideas for other Revolutionary War points of view to explore:

* King George and the British parliament decided which laws to pass and how to enforce them. What was it like to rule a colony from across the ocean?

* Wives of patriot soldiers had to run farms and businesses without their husbands. What would daily life be like for patriot women?

* Colonists relied on letters, newspapers, and messengers to get information. How would citizens in Boston spread word of the battle? What was it like to be in Philadelphia waiting for news?

READ MORE

Anderson, Dale. *The Causes of the American Revolution.* Milwaukee: World Almanac Library, 2006.

Englar, Mary. *The Battle of Bunker Hill.* Minneapolis: Compass Point Books, 2007.

Ingram, Scott. *The Battle of Bunker Hill.* San Diego: Blackbirch Press, 2004.

Waldman, Scott P. *The Battle of Bunker Hill.* New York: PowerKids Press, 2003.

INTERNET SITES

FactHound offers a safe, fun way to find Internet sites related to this book. All of the sites on FactHound have been researched by our staff.

Here's how:

1. Visit *www.facthound.com*
2. Choose your grade level.
3. Type in this book ID **1429601590** for age-appropriate sites. You may also browse subjects by clicking on letters, or by clicking on pictures and words.
4. Click on the **Fetch It** button.

FactHound will fetch the best sites for you!

GLOSSARY

ammunition (am-yuh-NISH-uhn)—objects fired from guns

artillery (ar-TIL-uh-ree)—cannons and other large guns used during battles

cartridge (KAR-trij)—a paper tube holding a ball and gunpowder used in muskets

colonist (KOL-uh-nist)—someone who lives in a newly settled area.

infantry (IN-fuhn-tree)—soldiers who march on the ground and carry guns

militia (muh-LISH-uh)—a part-time military force composed of local citizens

110

parliament (PAR-luh-muhnt)—people who have been elected to make laws in some countries

redoubt (rih-DOUT)—a small fort made of dirt

regiment (REJ-uh-muhnt)—a large group of soldiers who fight together as a unit

reinforcements (ree-in-FORSS-muhnts)—extra troops sent into battle

siege (SEEJ)—the surrounding of a city by troops to cut off movement in or out

BIBLIOGRAPHY

Barker, John. *The British in Boston: Being the Diary of Lieutenant John Barker of the King's Own Regiment from November 1774 to May 31, 1776.* Notes by Elizabeth Ellery Dana. Cambridge: Harvard University Press, 1924.

Brooks, Victor. *The Boston Campaign.* Conshohocken, Penn.: Combined Publishing, 1999.

Cary, John. *Joseph Warren: Physician, Politician, Patriot.* Urbana, Ill.: University of Illinois Press, 1961.

Curtis, Edward E. *The Organization of the British Army in the American Revolution.* Reprint. New York: AMS Press, 1969.

Frothingham, Richard. *History of the Siege of Boston, and of the Battles of Lexington, Concord, and Bunker Hill.* Reprint. New York: Da Capo Press, 1970.

Ketchum, Richard M. *Decisive Day: The Battle for Bunker Hill.* Garden City, N.Y.: Doubleday & Company, 1974.

Morrissey, Brendan. *Boston 1775: The Shot Heard Around the World.* Westport, Conn.: Praeger, 2004.

Index

Battles of Lexington and
    Concord, 6, 9, 106
Boston, 7, 8, 72, 73, 88, 101,
    106, 107
    siege of, 11, 15, 76, 88, 105
Breed's Hill, 18, 29, 83, 87, 107
Bunker Hill, 17, 24, 35, 43, 68,
    69, 83

Cambridge, 11, 13, 18, 78, 83,
    90
Charlestown, 30, 45, 47, 78, 83,
    97, 98, 100, 107
Clinton, General Henry, 46, 60,
    62, 103
Connecticut regiment, 18, 22,
    29, 31, 32
Continental Congress, 104,
    105, 106

Dorchester, 15, 76, 103, 105,
    106, 107

Gage, General Thomas, 9, 88,
    103, 104, 106
George, King, 8
Gridley, Richard, 18

Howe, General William, 46, 47,
    51, 58, 59

Loyalists, 8, 73, 76, 84, 85, 88,
    89, 99

Massachusetts regiment, 29,
    31, 83

New Hampshire regiment, 22,
    29, 31, 32

Pigot, General Robert, 47, 62
Pollard, Asa, 20, 26
Prescott, Colonel William, 17,
    18, 19, 20, 34, 37
Putnam, General Israel, 18, 43,
    104

rail fence, 29, 39, 59, 97
redoubt, 17, 18, 32, 33, 43, 45,
    63, 86, 100, 103, 107
Ruggles, General Timothy, 99,
    100

Stark, Colonel John, 39, 40,
    41, 42
stone wall, 29, 31, 39, 49

Ward, General Artemus, 11, 17
Warren, Dr. Joseph, 22, 23, 37,
    104